easy origami

EASY
Origami
TOYS

by christopher L. Harbo

CAPSTONE PRESS
a capstone imprint

First Facts is published by Capstone Press,
151 Good Counsel Drive, P.O. Box 669, Mankato, Minnesota 56002.
www.capstonepub.com

 Books published by Capstone Press are manufactured with paper
containing at least 10 percent post-consumer waste.

Library of Congress Cataloging-in-Publication Data
Harbo, Christopher L.
  Easy origami toys / by Christopher L. Harbo.
     p. cm.—(First facts. Easy origami)
  Includes bibliographical references.
  ISBN 978-1-4296-5386-2 (library binding)
  1. Origami—Juvenile literature. 2. Paper toy making—Juvenile literature. I. Title. II. Series.

TT870.H3223 2011
736'.982—dc22   2010024788

Editorial Credits
Designer: ALISON THIELE
Photo Studio Specialist: SARAH SCHUETTE
Scheduler: MARCY MORIN
Production Specialist: LAURA MANTHE

Photo Credits
Capstone Studio/Karon Dubke, all photos

Artistic Effects
Shutterstock/ Jackie Stukey, Nebojsa I, oorka, patrimonio designs limited,
   Petr Bukal, Skocko, SoleilC

ABOUT THE AUTHOR

Christopher L. Harbo loves origami. He began folding
paper several years ago and hasn't quit since. In
addition to decorative origami, he also enjoys folding
paper airplanes. When he's not practicing origami,
Christopher spends his free time reading Japanese
comic books and watching movies.

Printed in the United States of America in North Mankato, Minnesota.
092010   005933CGS11

TABLE OF Contents

ORIGAMI Toy Box

Peek inside the origami toy box! You'll find a treasure chest loaded with seven fun paper toys. Practice your jump shot with a clever basketball hoop. Send a pair of paper sumo wrestlers into battle. Challenge your friends to bug-eyed darting frog races. Jump in, start folding, and let the fun begin!

MATERIALS

Origami is a simple art that doesn't use many materials. You'll only need the following things to complete the projects in this book:

Ruler: Some models use measurements to complete. A ruler will help you measure.

Origami Paper: Square origami paper comes in many fun colors and sizes. You can buy this paper in most craft stores.

Letter-sized Paper: Not all origami models begin with a square. Use 8.5- by 11-inch (22- by 28-centimeter) paper when needed.

Pencil: Use a pencil when you need to mark spots you measure with the ruler.

Craft Supplies: Markers and other craft supplies will help you decorate your models.

FOLDING TECHNIQUES

Folding paper is easier when you understand basic origami folds and symbols. Practice the folds on this list before trying the models in this book. Turn back to this list if you get stuck on a tricky step, or ask an adult for help.

Valley Folds are represented by a dashed line. One side of the paper is folded against the other like a book. A sharp fold is made by running your finger along the fold line.

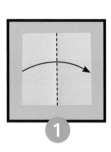
1

2

3

4

1

2

3

4

Mountain Folds are represented by a pink or white dashed and dotted line. The paper is folded sharply behind the model.

Squash Folds are formed by lifting one edge of a pocket. The pocket gets folded again so the spine gets flattened. The existing fold lines become new edges.

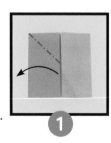
1

2

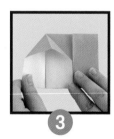
3

4

1

2

3

4

Inside reverse folds are made by opening a pocket slightly. Then you fold the model inside itself along existing fold lines.

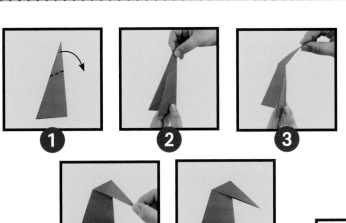

Outside reverse folds are made by opening a pocket slightly. Then you fold the model outside itself along existing fold lines.

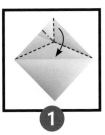  

Rabbit ear folds are formed by bringing two edges of a point together using existing fold lines. The new point is folded to one side.

SYMBOLS

SINGLE-POINTED ARROW:
Fold the paper in the direction of the arrow.

HALF-POINTED ARROW:
Fold the paper behind.

DOUBLE-POINTED ARROW:
Fold the paper and then unfold it.

LOOPING ARROW:
Turn the paper over or turn it to a new position.

BASKETBALL Hoop

Traditional Model

Get ready to shoot some hoops without ever leaving the table. Fold this basketball hoop and hold a free throw contest.

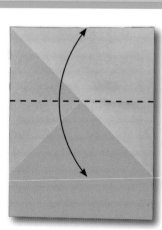

1

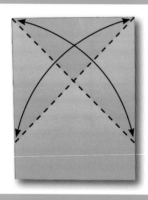

Start with a letter-sized piece of paper. Valley fold the top-left corner to the right edge and unfold. Valley fold the top-right corner to the left edge and unfold.

Turn the paper over.

2

Valley fold the top edge down and unfold. Note that the corners should meet the ends of the folds from step 1.

3

4

Turn the paper over.

5

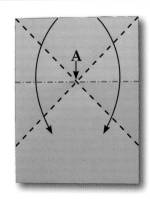

Use your finger to push down on the paper at point A. Grab the top edge of the paper and pull it toward the bottom on the fold lines. The top layer of the paper will form a triangle.

6

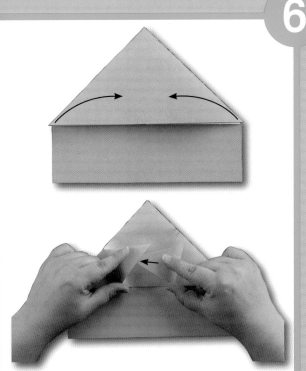

Curl the left and right points of the triangle toward each other. Tuck one point inside the other to form a hoop.

7

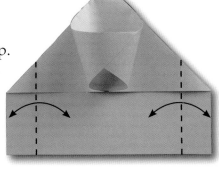

Valley fold the left and right edges even with the sides of the hoop. Then unfold the edges halfway.

8

Game on! Crumple a piece of paper into a ball and take your best shot at the hoop.

PLAY Hint Place your hoop on the end of a long table. Practice shooting baskets from the other end of the table. See how many baskets you can make in a row.

HUNGRY Crow

Traditional Model

A hungry crow will search high and low for a meal. This model walks across the table as it pecks for food.

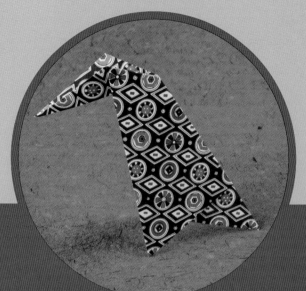

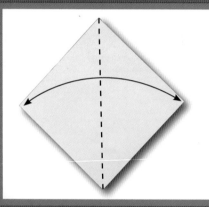

1

Start with the colored side of the paper face down. Valley fold the left point to the right point and unfold.

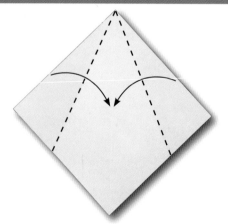

Valley fold the top-left edge to the center. Valley fold the top-right edge to the center.

2

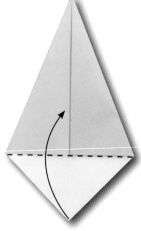

Valley fold the bottom point up. Make this fold along the edge made in step 2.

3

4

Valley fold the point past the bottom edge. Make this fold about .5 inch (1.3 cm) from the model's bottom edge.

5

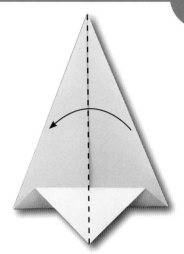

Valley fold the right side of the model to the left side.

6

Valley fold the top point down and to the left. Run your finger firmly along the fold and then unfold the point.

7

Reverse fold the point on the folds from step 6. This fold allows the right edge of the point to swing inside the model. When finished, the point sticks out from the left side of the model.

Peck, peck, peck. Your hungry crow is ready to eat.

8

PLAY Hint Tilt the crow so its beak rests on the table. Gently tap its tail to make the hungry crow walk and peck.

11

ROYAL Crown

Traditional Model

Kings and queens need crowns to rule their kingdoms. Fold this simple model, and your royal head will never be bare.

1

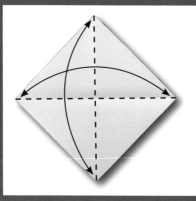

Start with the colored side of the paper face down. Valley fold the left point to the right point and unfold. Valley fold the top point to the bottom point and unfold.

2

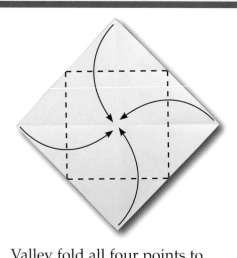

Valley fold all four points to the center of the paper.

3

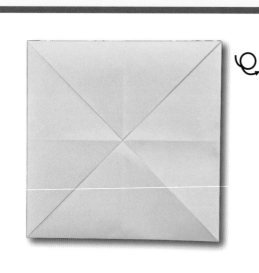

Turn the model over.

4

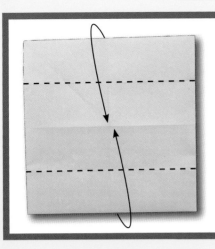

Valley fold the top and bottom edges to the center fold. Allow the flaps behind the edges to swing to the front.

5

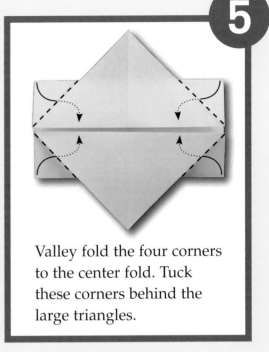

Valley fold the four corners to the center fold. Tuck these corners behind the large triangles.

6

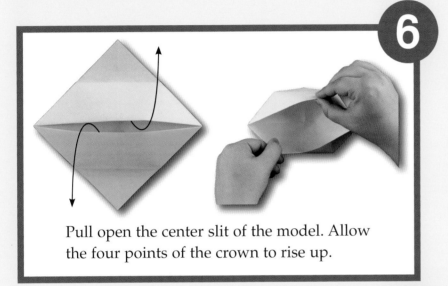

Pull open the center slit of the model. Allow the four points of the crown to rise up.

7

Pinch the crown's corners to make the model square.

Wear your crown to be a king or queen for the day!

8

PLAY Hint To wear this crown, be sure you start with a piece of paper large enough to fit your head. An 18-inch (46-cm) square of newspaper works best.

 13

AIR Shark

Traditional Model

The air shark is no ordinary paper airplane. It hunts the skies with a large fin rising up from its back.

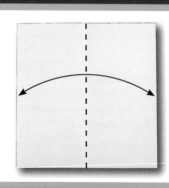

1 Start with the colored side of the paper face down. Valley fold the left edge to the right edge and unfold.

2 Valley fold the top-left corner to the center fold. Valley fold the top-right corner to the center fold.

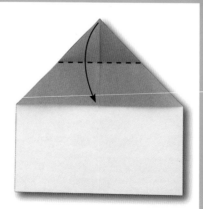

3 Valley fold the top point to the edge made in step 2.

Valley fold the top-left edge to the center. Valley fold the top-right edge to the center.

4

5

Mountain fold the right side of the model behind the left side. Then turn the model so the tip points to the right.

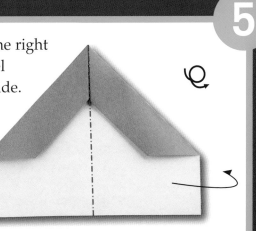

6

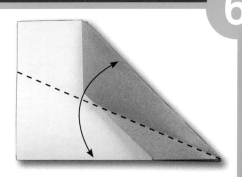

Valley fold the top wing to the bottom edge and unfold. Repeat this step on the back wing.

7

Valley fold the bottom-left corner up. Note how the corner meets the top flap's short edge. Make a firm fold and then unfold.

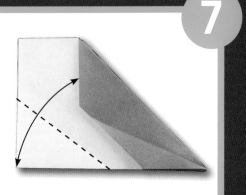

8

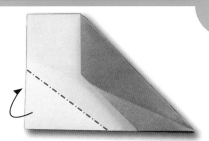

Reverse fold the bottom-left corner on the folds from step 7. This fold allows the bottom edge to swing inside the model.

9

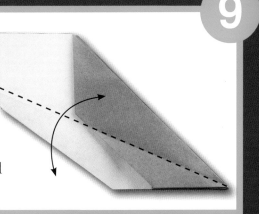

Valley fold both wings on the folds from step 6. Unfold the wings halfway.

10

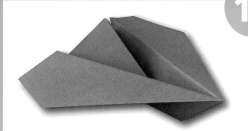

You've earned your wings! Give your plane a test flight.

PLAY Hint Pinch the bottom of the air shark with your fingers. Send it soaring with a smooth, level throw.

MINI Piano

Traditional Model

Dress up your dollhouse with a mini piano. Make it fancy by folding it in black paper. Or try red, green, or yellow paper for a fun, playful look.

1

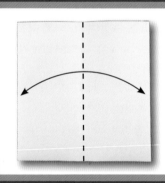

Start with the colored side of the paper face down. Valley fold the left edge to the right edge and unfold.

2

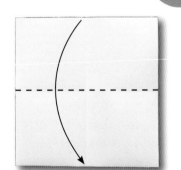

Valley fold the top edge to the bottom edge.

3

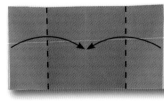

Valley fold the left and right edges to the center fold. You now have two tall flaps on top of the model.

4

Take the left flap and valley fold its top inside corner to the left edge. Make a firm fold and then unfold. Repeat this step on the right flap.

5

Squash fold the left flap. Make this fold by flattening the top inside corner on the folds from step 4. Repeat this step on the right flap.

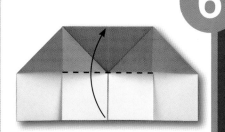

6

Take the top layer and valley fold its bottom edge to the model's top edge.

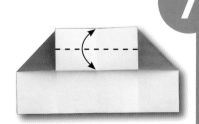

7

Take the top layer and valley fold its top edge to the middle edge. Make a firm fold and unfold.

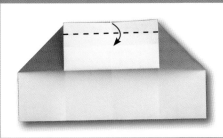

8

Valley fold the top layer again. This time the top edge meets the fold from step 7.

9

Valley fold the top layer one more time. This fold is made on the fold from step 7.

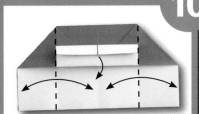

10

Valley fold the left and right edges to the center fold. Unfold the edges halfway. Then lower the top layer to form the keyboard.

11

Your mini piano is ready for its keys. Draw the piano keys with a black marker.

PLAY Hint Pretend one of your dolls is giving a concert in the park. Do you need seating for the other dolls? Make a second model, but don't color in the keys. This model can serve as a park bench.

SUMO Wrestler

Traditional Model

You don't have to visit Japan to see the power of sumo wrestlers. Fold your own wrestlers, and let them battle it out in the ring!

1

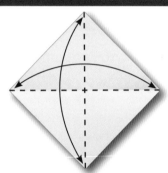

Start with the colored side of the paper face down. Valley fold the left point to the right point and unfold. Valley fold the top point to the bottom point and unfold.

2

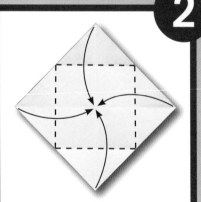

Valley fold all four corners to the center of the paper. The folds will form a smaller square.

3

Valley fold all four corners of the smaller square to the center of the paper.

4

Turn the model over.

5

Valley fold the top-left edge to the center fold. Allow the flap behind the edge to swing to the front. Repeat this step on the top-right edge.

6

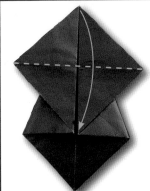

Valley fold the top point down to meet the middle point. Allow the flap behind the point to swing to the front.

7

Mountain fold the bottom point behind the model.

8

Valley fold the right side of the model to the left side.

9

Valley fold the triangle-shaped flap at the bottom of the model. Make this fold by opening the left side of the model and pulling the tip of the flap down. Then close the model and allow the flap to valley fold in half.

10

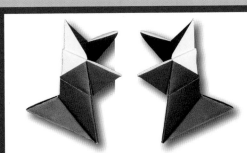

Your sumo wrestler is ready to rumble!

PLAY Hint

Draw a large circle in the middle of a notebook. Place two sumo wrestlers in the center of the circle. Slide one end of the notebook over the edge of the table. Tap the overhanging part of the notebook rapidly. The first wrestler to fall down or cross the edge of the circle loses the match.

BUG-EYED Darting Frog

Traditional Model

The bug-eyed darting frog would rather run than hop. This model is built for speed and is ready to race!

1 Start with the colored side of the paper face down. Valley fold the bottom-left edge to the top-right edge and unfold. Valley fold the bottom-right edge to the top-left edge and unfold.

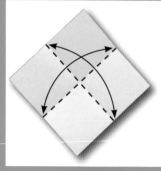

2 Valley fold all four points to the center of the paper to form a smaller square.

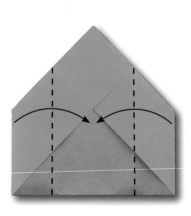

4 Valley fold the left and right edges to the center of the model.

3 Mountain fold the top corners behind the model. The corners should meet the center of the model.

 **20**

5

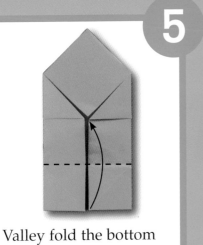

Valley fold the bottom edge to the center edge.

6

Valley fold the corners of the top layer to the bottom edge.

7

Pinch the tops of the triangles from step 6. Gently pull the top layers of these triangles out to the sides of the model. Two pointed feet will form.

8

Turn the model over.

9

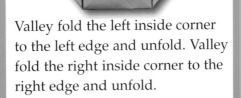

Valley fold the left inside corner to the left edge and unfold. Valley fold the right inside corner to the right edge and unfold.

10

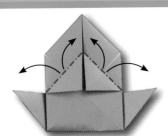

Open the slit of the left inside corner. Squash fold on the folds from step 9 to form a rectangle-shaped eye. Repeat this step on the right inside corner.

11

The race is on! See how fast your bug-eyed darting frog can run.

PLAY Hint Place two frogs side-by-side on a table. At the same time, you and a friend must blow on the back ends of your frogs. The first frog to dart all the way across the table wins.

READ More

Boonyadhistarn, Thiranut. *Origami: The Fun and Funky Art of Paper Folding.* Crafts. Mankato, Minn.: Capstone Press, 2007.

Boursin, Didier. *Folding for Fun.* Richmond Hill, Ont.: Firefly Books, 2007.

Engel, Peter. *10-Fold Origami: Fabulous Paperfolds You Can Make in 10 Steps or Less.* New York: Sterling Pub. Co. Inc., 2008.

Meinking, Mary. *Easy Origami.* Origami. Mankato, Minn.: Capstone Press, 2009.

Shingu, Fumiaki. *Easy Origami.* New York: Mud Puddle Books, 2007.

INTERNET Sites

FactHound offers a safe, fun way to find Internet sites related to this book. All of the sites on FactHound have been researched by our staff.

Here's all you do:

Visit *www.facthound.com*

Type in this code: 9781429653862

Check out projects, games and lots more at
www.capstonekids.com

5/2011